THE ESCAPE AND CAPTURE
OF
JOHN WILKES BOOTH

by EDWARD STEERS, JR.

Abraham Lincoln. 1809 - 1865. Assassination was not new to Lincoln. During his four years in the White House Lincoln had personally received over one hundred letters detailing his proposed murder. At least two other bonafide plots to kidnap him had preceded Booth's attempt of March 17, 1865. Would a successful abduction of Lincoln have ultimately saved his life and changed history?

THE MURDER

April 14th dawned as a special day for Washington City. The drizzle which had covered the capital for the past two days had failed to dampen the spirits of the local citizenry in their celebration of Lee's surrender on April 9th. It was Good Friday and neither the weather nor the religious importance of this holy day had affected the jubilation that ran through the streets of the capital city.

The evening show scheduled at John Ford's theatre on 10th Street was filled to capacity for the benefit performance of the celebrated Laura Keene, but the truth of the matter was that most of the people in attendance that evening had come to catch a glimpse of the President and General Ulysses Grant whose attendance had been well advertised in the afternoon papers.

Grant, General in Chief of all of the Union forces had arrived in town the day before to attend to the necessary paperwork associated with the long awaited surrender of Lee's Army of Northern Virginia. In mid-morning, on the fourteenth, he had attended the regularly scheduled cabinet meeting as the President's guest where he received the congratulations of Lincoln's chief advisors. Not all of them were fans of Grant, to be sure, but whatever opposition had existed had been crushed along with Southern independence at Appomattox five days earlier. Grant was the North's great hero and stood alone at the pinnacle of national adoration.

Lincoln was more than pleased to give Grant his due and present him publicly to the grateful country. At the cabinet meeting that morning, Lincoln extended an invitation to the General and his wife to attend the evening performance at Ford's starring Laura Keene in a British spoof on their bumpkin cousins, the Americans. No president, before or since, enjoyed a self-deprecating joke more than Abraham Lincoln. His humility was as tall as his figure and he laughed heartily at a good joke, especially one whose object was himself.

Interestingly, the invitation to Grant to visit the theatre with the President was not the first. On February 10, just two months before, Lincoln had visited Ford's for the evening performance of a play entitled "Love in Livery" in which Booth's own brother-in-law, John Sleeper Clarke, was starring. At this performance Ulysses Grant and Ambrose Burnside had accompanied the President and the three men watched the play from the Presidential Box. Grant had come to Washington that day to attend to the reinstatement of prisoner

3

John Ford's theatre located on Tenth Street between E and F. Lincoln had attended Ford's on eleven occasions that we know of. He had seen John Wilkes Booth perform here in 1863 and had attended a performance with General Grant in February of 1865 only eight weeks before the night of his assassination.

Charles Forbes, personal attendent to Lincoln and close friend of the family was seated in the fourth row, end seat, directly outside the box when John Wilkes Booth approached him. No statement or affidavit from Forbes was taken and we do not know what Booth said to him or what was written on the card Booth gave to him.

The beautiful and brilliant Laura Keene. April 14 was the last night of her star appearance at Ford's. Lincoln had come to see her special benefit performance in which she would receive the box office revenues as her payment.

Mary Todd Lincoln. 1818 - 1882. Dressed in mourning black in memory of her eleven year old son William Wallace Lincoln, known as Willie, who died in the White House in February of 1862. Mary Lincoln's temper and fits of abusive anger were well known to Lincoln's friends and close advisors. An outburst against Julia Dent Grant in February of 1865 in all probability convinced Mrs. Grant not to attend the theatre with the Lincolns on the night of April 14.

exchange. A move he felt he could now afford with Lee at bay. The three men attended the performance without their wives.

Now, two months later and five days after the unofficial end of the war, Grant happily accepted Lincoln's invitation to attend the theatre again, this time with their wives. Word was sent to Ford's that the party would need the Presidential box for the President and the General. Harry Ford, John Ford's younger brother and business partner, immediately sent word to the local papers announcing the planned visit by the country's two great heroes. It would insure a sellout. As it turned out, Grant cancelled the invitation later in the day at the insistence of his wife. Julia Dent Grant had experienced the ungracious behavior of Mary Todd Lincoln several weeks before at a review of the Army of the James and it left a chilling feeling with the General's lady. She decided instead that she and the General would take the afternoon train to visit their children in New Jersey. Unbeknownst to the public, Grant would not show at the theatre, but the President would and he was riding the euphoria of Union victory. Lincoln was still a big draw and the loyal public would come out to see him with or without Grant.

The Lincoln's finally were able to get another couple to join them and decided to keep their appointment. Mary Lincoln insisted that the President needed the distraction from the stress of his office. Major Henry Rathbone and his fiancee, Clara Harris joined the couple for a relaxing night out.

Just as the perceptive Ford brothers had guessed, it was a sellout crowd for the evening performance. Among those who had come to Ford's Theatre just to see the President that Good Friday was John Wilkes Booth. But unlike most of those in attendance, Booth's interest in Lincoln did not stem from admiration; his purpose that holy day was murder.

Ticket issued for the performance of Friday, April 14, 1865. Issued by James R. Ford. James Ford was brother to John and Harry Clay Ford and served as business manager of the theatre.

It was a few minutes past nine p.m. when Booth rode his mare into the dark alley leading up to the rear door of the theatre. As he approached the back of the building the sound of his little mare's hooves resonated off of the wooden shanties that lined the alley. There was a damp chill in the air which went completely unnoticed by the famous actor. Booth hesitated for a moment before dismounting, his dark eyes carefully studying the large, brick edifice in front of him. He had frequented this theatre many times and was well versed in its configuration and that of the alley. John Ford had given him virtual run of the property and even held the actor's mail for him as a courtesy to his star status.

John Wilkes Booth, like his famous father and brother before him, had quickly ascended to the heights of the American stage in the short span of the war years. Although he had gotten off to an inauspicious start and was probably unfairly compared to his famous father and brother, he quickly rebounded and became a matinee idol of star quality. His income from acting in 1864 was purported to

A rear view of Ford's Theatre. The door through which Booth entered the theatre and through which he fled following his act. The alley was known as *Baptist Alley* from the days when the building housed the *Tenth Street Baptist Church*.

approximate $20,000 which was equivalent to a small fortune even during the inflation years of the war. At 26 years old, Booth was handsome, intelligent and rich. Attributes that most people would kill for. Booth, however, had other reasons.

Dismounting his small mare, he called to one of the stagehands near the rear door, Edman Spangler, who he told to hold his horse while he went into the theatre. Spangler, who worked at the theatre as a stagehand and sometimes carpenter, was already busy with the ongoing play. Spangler was a friend of Booth's, perhaps from the days when he helped build the elder Booth's home in Bel Aire, Maryland. He obediently took the reins of Booth's horse and watched the man quietly enter into the rear of the theatre. Shortly after Booth had disappeared inside, Spangler passed the job onto a young boy by the name of "Peanuts" Burroughs, who worked at the theatre attending to small tasks.

Entering into the backstage area of the theatre, Booth quietly lifted a trapdoor cut into the floor in the right hand corner of the back stage area and descended down a flight of wooden steps which led to a dirt cellar directly beneath the stage. Passing under the stage to the opposite side, he came up a second set of stairs. By this maneuver, Booth was able to pass from the right side of the rear stage to the left side without disturbing the performers or stagehands busy at their work. Even if he had been noticed it would have passed without incident.

From his position at the left rear of the stage he was now able to pass through a stagedoor which opened onto a narrow alley running between the theatre and an adjoining bar, appropriately named, the Star Saloon. Booth exited onto the sidewalk in front of the theatre and went into the adjoining saloon. His familiarity with the intricacies of Ford's had allowed him to move from the rear of the theatre to its front without disturbing the play in progress or even being noticed. This also allowed him to leave his horse carefully attended to in the rear of the theatre by his friend, Edman Spangler, or so he thought. Booth's only avenue of escape would be from through the back door into the dark alleyway known locally as *Baptist Alley*, a carryover from when the theatre had been the 10th Street Baptist Church.

After downing a brandy and exchanging small talk with the saloonkeeper, Booth entered the lobby of the theatre through the front door where he passed the ticket agent, Joseph Sessford, with a brief nod of his head. It was approximately 10:00 p.m. as he slowly moved across the front lobby from the ticket door on the right toward the staircase at the far left which lead to the dress circle and boxes above.

The Star Saloon. The saloon was separated from the theatre by a small alley way which ran between the two buildings. It was operated by a man named Peter Taltavul who exchanged small talk with Booth before he entered the theatre.

Edman Spangler. ? - 1871. Tried as a conspirator in Lincoln's murder, Spangler received the lightest sentence of all, six years. He was pardoned along with Mudd and Arnold after serving three years. He returned home with Mudd and spent the last two years of his life living at the Mudd home. He is buried in old St. Peter's cemetery near Beantown.

9

He carefully ascended the staircase leading to the dress circle and began moving across the rear promenade that led to the box holding President Lincoln. He had to traverse the entire rear of the dress circle to reach the aisle leading to the box. The theatre was sold out and the overflow crowd was standing along the entire rear of the promenade. This forced Booth to pass in front of the standing crowd now entranced by the performance below.

As he approached the box, Booth did a curious thing according to witnesses who testified later at the conspiracy trial. Booth paused at a man seated in the end chair of the fourth row not more than a few feet from the outer door to the box. As if by established procedure, he reached into his vest pocket and withdrawing a small "card" presented it to the man. This man had accompanied the Lincoln's to the theatre. His name was Charles Forbes. Forbes was the President's valet and a personal friend of the Lincolns who attended to many family needs at the White House. He had positioned himself close to the door leading to the President's box and was apparently recognized by Booth who stopped at his side before proceeding into the box.

Also accompanying the President to the theatre that evening, but absent from a position by the door, was John F. Parker, a member of the Washington Metropolitan police force assigned to the White House as one of the President's four bodyguards. Parker had assumed his post earlier in the evening relieving the daytime guard, William Crook.

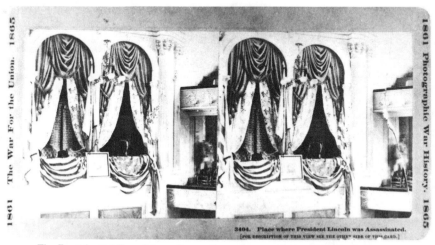

The Presidential Box. Normally configured as two boxes a single, large box was created by removing a center partition. Ford had placed a rocker, settee and side chair from his own office in the box for the President and his guests.

Charles Forbes, 1835 - 1895. Personal valet to the President, Forbes was sitting outside the box when Booth approached. Evidence indicates that he waved Booth into the box after a brief exchange. He is buried in Congressional Cemetery in Washington in what had been an unmarked grave. The Lincoln Group of D.C. placed a head stone on his grave in 1984 with an epitaph identifying his connection with Lincoln.

Stereograph of the Lincoln Rocker. ca.1865. Originally seized by the government, John Ford's widow eventually secured the return of the chair and promptly sold it to Henry Ford for his museum in Deerfield.

Most historians have concluded that Parker's place should have been at the door of the box near where Charles Forbes was seated. He was not there, however, when Booth approached. His exact whereabouts remain unclear, but it is just as likely that he was viewing the play from the rear promenade as it is that he was off in a saloon drinking. Parker was later charged with negligence by a police board of inquiry, but was apparently exonerated when a special hearing resulted in all of the charges against him being dismissed. Unfortunately for historians, the testimony and proceedings of the hearing were held *sub rosa* and no known record exists today. Whether it was Parker's duty to station himself at the door to the box during the performance or simply to accompany Lincoln to and from the theatre has never been established. In any event, he was absent from the door, but Charles Forbes was not, at least he was close enough to engage Booth momentarily. Interestingly, Forbes never appeared at the trial of the conspirators nor left a statement which history is aware of. He was, however, the accuser of John Parker on the charges later filed by the Police Department claiming Parker was negligent.

Testimony indicates that Booth presented Forbes with a card on which he had made a notation. Whether Forbes kept the card or returned it to Booth is not known. After this brief exchange with Forbes, however, Booth entered the box, closed the door behind him

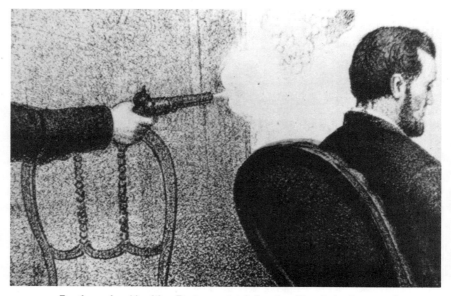

Booth used a .44 caliber Deringer pistol shooting Lincoln in the rear of the head at point blank range.

and secured it with a wooden bar fashioned earlier in the day from a music stand. It was now approximately 10:20 p.m. and the play in progress had reached a point where actor Harry Hawk stood alone on stage reciting his now famous comic lines.

Booth had gained the access he needed to carry out his murderous plan. As he stood in the darkened hallway before the final door leading into the box, a shaft of yellow light fell against the pocket of his coat marking the bulge caused by the small pistol hidden there. The light came from a small hole which had carefully been drilled above the knob of the door separating Booth from the President. Flushed, Booth's heart began to beat forcibly as he stared at the yellow spot on the black cloth. With one hand he slowly removed the small derringer from his coat pocket breaking up the pattern of reflected light. With his other hand he withdrew a large bowie knife from his waistband. Booth then carefully opened the inner door to the box, stepped inside and raising the pistol a few inches from the President, fired a small leaden ball into the back of Lincoln's head at the precise moment the audience erupted in loud laughter.

For a moment, everyone froze not comprehending the event. Lincoln slumped toward his wife who was sitting to his right holding his hand in hers. As the acrid smoke from the derringer filled her nostrils, she began screaming as she clutched the limp body in her arms. Rathbone, realizing the situation, jumped to his feet and grabbed the assailant. In the ensuing scuffle, Booth stabbed Rathbone in the upper arm and breaking away from his grip, vaulted over the flag draped balustrade onto the stage below. Catching his spur in a flag as he cleared the railing, Booth landed off balance on the stage fracturing the small bone in his left leg.

While in the box and later on stage, various witnesses have testified that Booth shouted to the audience. Included were the dramatic lines found on Virginia's state seal, *Sic Semper Tyrannis - Thus Always to Tyrants*. Booth's flair for the dramatic was always present, and in his mind he had just played his greatest role.

Gathering himself up from where he landed, Booth turned to his right and pushing aside the lone actor on stage, Harry Hawk, limped across the stage and past actress Jenny Gourlay and orchestra leader William Withers who were conversing in the narrow passageway backstage. Booth rushed through the rear stage door and lunging forward, desperately looked for his horse which he had left there some ninety minutes before. Lying on a wooden bench with the reins in his hand was the young boy who Spangler had turned the horse sitting task over to. Tearing the reins from the startled boys grip, Booth knocked him to the ground with the butt of his bowie knife as the boy started to rise up from the bench. Swinging onto the mare, Booth

To *John F. Parker*

SIR: Take notice that charges have been preferred against you, to the Board of Metropolitan Police, which charges are now on file in the office of the Secretary of the Board, at No. 483 "Tenth" street, and a copy thereof is hereto annexed. You are hereby notified and required to answer the said charges in accordance with, and in the manner required by, the Rules and Regulations for the Government of the Police Force.

You will also take notice that your trial upon said charges will be in order, and will take place, at a meeting of this Board to be held at the office of the said Board, No. 483 "Tenth" street, in said city, on the *third* day of *May*, 1865, at *1* o'clock p. m., and will be continued from day to day until the trial is concluded.

T. A. Lazenby, Secretary.

To the Board of Metropolitan Police:

I hereby CHARGE *Patrolman John F. Parker of the 5th Precinct*

with *Neglect of duty.*

SPECIFICATION.

In this, that Said Parker was detailed to attend and protect the President Mr. Lincoln, that while the President was at Fords Theatre on the night of the 14 of April last, Said Parker allowed a man to enter the President's private Box and Shoot the President

Respectfully,
A. C. Richards
Supt

Witnesses

A. C. Richards

Supt Furbo at President's House

I ADMIT due personal service on me of copies of the within complaint, charges, specifications, and notice of trial, this *1st* day of *May*, 1865.

John F. Parker.

wheeled the horse about and galloped the few feet down the darkened alley, turning sharply into the public alley that led up to F Street. On reaching F Street he turned east in the direction of the Capitol.

The handsome and debonair actor had come to the theatre a little over an hour before, a highly respected and successful thespian. Now he was to begin a desperate and painful escape, a hunted and disgraced man. If his moment of glory was fleeting, his infamy would be eternal.

This edition of the *Tribune* was printed so soon after word of the assassination (2:30 a.m. edition) that the first account of events appears on page 4. It is this edition that Laura Keene identifies the assassin as John Wilkes Booth.

Photocopy of the charge and specification filed by the Metropolitan Police Board against John F. Parker, Lincoln's bodyguard on the night of April 14. The specification reads in part that the *said Parker allowed a man to enter the Presedent's (sic) private box and shoot the President.* Parker's trial was held on May 3, 1865, at which time he was acquitted of all charges and reinstated. He was subsequently dismissed from the force in 1868 for dereliction of duty in another unrelated matter.

Joseph Sessford. Sessford served as John Ford's ticket agent. On the night of April 14, he passed Booth into the theatre. Sessford was well acquainted with the famous actor and knew that he had free access to the theatre as one of its star performers.

Lawrence Gobright. A reporter for the Associated Press, Gobright found Booth's fatal derringer on the floor of the box while searching for his apartment key the day after the assassination. He turned it over to Stanton.

16

THE ESCAPE

Leaving confusion and hysteria behind him, Booth headed southeast toward the Navy Yard Bridge located at the end of 11th Street in southeast Washington. The bridge was the principal route leading from Washington into Maryland over the Eastern Branch (present day Anacostia) of the Potomac River. The exact route of Booth's flight to the bridge is not known, but a witness placed a lone man riding furiously along the south side of the Capitol, followed moments later by a second rider at approximately eleven p.m. that night. If indeed, the first rider was Booth, it seems probable that the second rider was a young man named Davy Herold.

Herold had been assigned by Booth to accompany Lewis (Paine) Powell in an attack on Secretary of State William Seward. Herold had waited outside the Seward home on Lafayette Square while Powell attempted to gain access to Seward. At the same moment that Booth was murdering the President, Powell was butchering the occupants of the Seward household. Powell had effectively disabled

The Navy Yard Bridge from Uniontown on the Maryland side looking back into the District.

one of Seward's sons, Frederick, Assistant Secretary of State, and was violently stabbing Seward as he lay in bed convalescing from a serious carriage accident which occurred the week before. Herold, waiting outside the house, had apparently become frightened at the screams and shouts coming from Seward house and panicked. Releasing the reins of Powell's horse, Herold galloped off at the sounds from Powell's bloody attack. He was spotted shortly afterward by stableman John Fletcher who managed the livery stables of Thompson Naylor located on E Street between 13th and 14th Streets. Herold had rented a horse from Fletcher earlier in the day and was now two hours overdue in returning it causing Fletcher some anxiety. Ironically, at the precise moment Herold was fleeing, Fletcher had walked the one block from his stables up to Pennsylvania looking for Herold when he saw him coming toward the Avenue down 15th Street. Recognizing Herold, Fletcher made a move toward him calling out to return the horse.

William Henry Seward. Secretary of State, 1861 - 1869. Seward was bed ridden recovering from a serious carriage accident in which his jaw suffered multiple fractures. Although knifed repeatedly by Paine, Seward eventually recovered and resumed his duties as Secretary of State. He was Lincoln's closest and most valued advisor who Booth felt shared responsibility with Lincoln for the war and its effect on the South.

Frederick Seward. The second oldest son of William Seward, Frederick served as his father's Assistant Secretary of State. On the night of Paine's attempted assassination of William Seward, Frederick was seriously injured by Paine suffering multiple skull fractures. He survived after a long convalescence.

George Andrew Atzerodt. 1835 - 1865.

Born in Thuringen, Germany, Atzerodt was recruited by Booth to ferry the kidnapped Lincoln over the Potomac. Assigned to assassinate Vice President Andrew Johnson at the Kirkwood Hotel, Atzerodt's courage evaporated at the last minute. Early Saturday morning he fled to the home of his cousin, Hartman Richter, in Germantown in Montgomery County, Maryland. Atzerodt was arrested on April 20 as Booth readied to cross the Potomac into Virginia. The hapless Atzerodt was one of four to hang on July 7, 1865.

Young Davy Herold. 1846 - 1865.

Often referred to as mentally slow, Herold was not. A careful reading of his statement taken following his arrest shows a cleverness not usually recognized by most authors. Accompanying Booth all the way, he was captured when Booth was killed and suffered the same fate as Atzerodt, Paine and Mary Surratt.

Herold, now trotting along the avenue, quickly spurred his horse and galloped up 14th Street toward F Street. Turning east onto F Street, he raced in the direction of the Navy Yard Bridge, only moments behind the escaping Booth.

Guarding the bridge on the evening of the fourteenth were three soldiers, Sergeant Silas T. Cobb and two privates. Wartime security was still in effect and while considerably relaxed as a result of Lee's surrender, passage into and out of Washington still required passing a military post.

Arriving at the bridge shortly before 11:00 p.m., Booth was challenged by Cobb. Here Booth did something very strange for a man trying to escape, he gave his real name and destination to the guards thereby leaving a crucial clue to the precise direction in which he was fleeing. Booth convinced Cobb that he was returning home to Beantown in southern Maryland, a small village close to where Booth and Herold would later pass on their way to Dr. Samuel A. Mudd's house. Mudd lived in the community known as *Beantown*. Certainly Booth could not have given testimony more helpful to a searching party.

Satisfied that the well-dressed gentleman posed no military threat, Cobb waved Booth across the bridge and returned to his conversation with his fellow soldiers. Within minutes a second rider galloped up and again Cobb was forced to challenge. Davy Herold, unlike Booth before him, gave an alias and said that he had inadvertently overstayed his visit with a certain *woman* in the city and was returning home to southern Maryland. The soldiers certainly could empathize with the horseman when it came to visiting women. An easy mistake to make. Once again Cobb waved the rider across the bridge and returned to his friends. For the third time within a span of several minutes a rider came galloping up to the bridge and for the third time Cobb challenged. This rider was John Fletcher who wasn't interested in leaving the city, only in pursuing a man who had stolen one of his horses. Cobb informed him that two riders had indeed passed over the bridge heading for southern Maryland and that Fletcher could also pass, but he would not be permitted to return until morning. Angered and discouraged at Cobb's ruling, Fletcher turned his horse about and headed back toward the center of town. Within the next two hours Fletcher was at General Augur's headquarters asking if anyone had turned in a stray horse.

Christopher Augur commanded the 22nd Army Corps and was in charge of the defenses around Washington. A shooting general, Augur had commanded a division in Louisiana under Nathaniel Banks during the siege of Port Hudson. As a result of his inquiries, Fletcher was shown a saddle which he positively identified as belonging to a

Christopher Columbus Augur. Augur had served in Louisiana with Bank's Army of the Gulf before coming to Washington and assuming command of the 22nd Army Corps. Augur reacted early on the morning of April 15 by sending a troop of the 13th New York Cavalry to Bryantown. Little did he realize that Booth was resting only five miles away from where the troops had set up their headquarters in Bryantown.

customer of his named G. A. Atzerodt. Atzerodt was further identified by Fletcher as an associate of Davy Herold who, it turned out, had stolen one of Fletchers horses and had ridden over the Navy Yard Bridge earlier that evening. Fletcher must have assumed that Davy Herold and George Atzerodt were the two men that had ridden over the Navy Yard bridge just a few hours earlier. By 2:00 a.m. General Augur's headquarters had evidence to link Herold to Atzerodt and a good suspicion that they had headed into Southern Maryland over the Navy Yard bridge. Most importantly, however, Atzerodt was directly linked to John Wilkes Booth later that morning by police detective John Lee, who Washington Provost Marshal James O'Beirne had sent to guard Vice President Andrew Johnson at the Kirkwood Hotel following the attack on Lincoln. On arriving at the Kirkwood, Lee was informed by the barkeeper, Michael Henry, that a *suspicious character* was occupying room 126. The suspicious character who had registered at the hotel was George Atzerodt. Atzerodt's assignment this bloody night was the assassination of Vice President Andrew Johnson who boarded at a room at the Kirkwood a short distance from the room taken by Atzerodt. Atzerodt had gone to the Kirkwood around 10 p.m., but as the critical moment approached, his courage evaporated and he quickly fled from the hotel bar. When Lee searched Atzerodt's room he found among several articles, a bankbook with the name "J. Wilkes Booth." Here was a positive link between three of the conspirators. Booth to Atzerodt and Atzerodt to Herold. And two of the three over the Navy Yard bridge into Southern Maryland.

After a brief delay, General Augur swung into action by sending a troop from the 13th New York Cavalry, under Lieutenant David D.

Andrew Johnson. 1808 - 1875. The Vice President was targeted by Booth for assassination at his room in the Kirkwood Hotel at Pennsylvania Avenue and 12th Street. Atzerodt came within a few feet and minutes of murdering Johnson but his courage evaporated at the last minute and he fled without carrying out his assignment.

Dana, over the Navy Yard Bridge and into Southern Maryland. By noon the next day, the 13th New York would be in Bryantown - only a few miles from the home of Dr. Samuel A. Mudd in the small community known as *Beantown*.

Crossing over the bridge into Uniontown located on the Maryland side of the river, Booth turned onto Good Hope Road and galloped up the steady incline passing between two of the sixty-nine forts and batteries that ringed Washington, Forts Wagner and Baker. It was near 11:30 p.m. and only now was Secretary of War Edwin M. Stanton setting up his command post in the Petersen House across from Ford's Theatre. Faulty research by some writers has led to the conclusion that the Navy Yard Bridge was the only avenue of escape from Washington left open to Booth, and that the military telegraph had been mysteriously shut down for several hours following the assassination. This was not true. A commercial telegraph, called the People's Line of Telegraph under the management of William H. Heiss, had been shorted out for two hours following Lincoln's assassination and deliberately so by Mr. Heiss. Heiss readily admitted that he closed down the commercial line as a patriotic act to prevent panic in outlying areas and to give the military and law enforcement authorities a head start on those who may otherwise act to hinder their pursuit. The military telegraph, however, was functioning the entire time sending and receiving telegrams at various intervals during the evening and morning hours.

The Navy Yard Bridge was not the only avenue of escape open to Booth that evening. The fact that he was permitted to pass by Sergeant Cobb was neither unique nor unusual. The military threat to Washington ended long before April 9, and after that date any reason for continued strict regulation of traffic had ended. On the day in question, April 14, Lincoln had written: *No pass is necessary now to authorize anyone to go to and return from Petersburg and Richmond - People go and return just as they did before the war. A. Lincoln.* And on April 1st a local newspaper *The Intelligencer* noted, *No Passes Required. On and after today, no more passes will be required to visit Alexandria.* It seems clear that the threat to the city had passed, and besides, Booth and Herold sought permission to leave the city, not enter it. Where is the threat in that?

Shortly after 11:30 p.m., Davy Herold and John Wilkes Booth met at a place called Soper's Hill some eight miles outside of the District line. Following their prearranged rendezvous, the pair headed for the tavern of Mary Surratt operated by Mr. John M. Lloyd, who rented the tavern from the widow.

John T. Ford. 1829 - 1894. Theatrical entrepreneur John T. Ford was the unfortunate owner of the theatre where Lincoln was shot. Confiscated by the government, Ford was eventually paid $100,000 for his theatre. He never again opened a theatre in the District.

Harry Clay Ford. The youngest of the three Ford brothers (born 1844), Harry served as treasurer for his brother's theatre business. It was Harry who secured the flags and decorated the box in anticipation of Lincoln and Grant's visit on the night of April 14.

James Reed Ford. Born 1840. Known to his family and friends as "Dick", James Ford served as Business Manager of the Tenth Street Theatre. His facsimile signature appeared on the back of all theatre tickets.

24

THE ROAD THROUGH MARYLAND

Situated thirteen miles southeast of Washington was the small village crossroads of Surrattsville where John H. Surratt, Sr. had operated a tavern and post office for many years until his death in 1862. After his father's death, John Surratt, Jr. had taken over his father's operation serving as postmaster for a brief period. By December of 1864, John's mother, Mary Surratt, decided to lease the Surrattsville property to John M. Lloyd for $500 a year and move into Washington where she operated a boarding house at 541 H Street N.W., a property owned by the Surratts since 1852. It was at this boarding house that several of the conspirators either stayed or met during the four months preceding the assassination and plotted their various abduction conspiracies. It was here that John Wilkes Booth came at noon on April 14 and held a private conversation with Mary Surratt and asked, among other things, that she take a special package to the tavern to Mr. Lloyd that very afternoon.

Following her meeting with the nice Mr. Booth, Mary Surratt left her H Street boarding house accompanied by one of her boarders, Louis Weichmann, and headed for Surrattsville. According to her later testimony, the purpose of her trip was to take care of some business she had with a man named John Nothey. Nothey had purchased 75 acres

The village crossroads of Surrattsville. The Surratt Tavern owned by Mary Surratt appears at the extreme left.

The Surratt Tavern as it appeared in the 1930's.

of land from John Surratt, Sr. several years before and never paid off his note. In need of money to settle a prior debt of her husband's, Mary Surratt claimed she went to Surrattsville on that fateful day to visit Nothey and collect the long overdue bill. Louis Weichman had been a schoolboy friend of John Surratt's and in coming to Washington had reestablished his acquaintance with his boyhood chum. Weichman has become one of the shadow figures in the assassination story being cast by some as an innocent and a devil by others.

According to Weichman, he became aware early on that something was up in the Surratt household and claims to have reported his suspicions to his immediate employer at the prison bureau. Others have suggested that he was not only aware of an abduction plot, but was a party to it. Whatever the truth, Weichman rushed to the authorities the minute he heard what had happened and became a member of the police effort in piecing together the people and events of that bloody night. If he was indeed a member of the conspiracy, he clearly acted effectively in disassociating himself from the pack. Contrary to the opinions of some, Weichman did not put the noose around Mary Surratt's neck, however, John Lloyd did. Weichman only helped to adjust it.

Before leaving Washington on the afternoon of April 14, Mrs. Surratt was visited by John Wilkes Booth during which time Booth gave her a small package and asked that she take it to Lloyd. This package later proved to contain a pair of field glasses which were picked up by the two fugitives that night on their escape from the city. Booth collared Weichman at the boarding house and giving him money, told him to rent a carriage and take Mary Surratt to the tavern. Following Booth's orders, the two of them arrived at the tavern in early evening and found the tavernkeeper Lloyd away at Marlboro where he was attending a trial. Rather than journey on to Nothey's, Mary Surratt decided to wait at the tavern for Lloyd's return. During her wait she made no attempt to see Nothey, but sent him a note which was written by Weichmann and delivered by a neighbor named Bennett Gwynn.

After a few hours, Lloyd returned from Marlboro. When he arrived at the tavern he went around to the rear of the house with his wagon, where he was met by Mary Surratt who had come out back to talk to him. At her trial, Lloyd testified that Mary Surratt told him to have the *shooting irons* ready; that they would be picked up later that evening by persons unnamed. The *shooting irons* which were referred to were not imaginary, they had been brought to the tavern a month earlier on March 17 by Davy Herold in anticipation of abducting Lincoln by Booth and his cohorts. At that time, Booth and his conspirators had planned to kidnap Lincoln while he was traveling to Campbell Hospital located midway between the capitol building in

Site of John C. Thompson's tavern at the little village crossroads of T.B. It was to this tavern that Davy Herold had come on March 17 after the failure of his cohorts to show up at the Surrattsville Tavern with the kidnapped President. Booth and Herold arrived at T.B. between 1:00 a.m. and 2:00 a.m. on the morning of April 15 and headed for the home of Dr. Samuel A. Mudd.

Lewis Paine alias Powell. Frequently characterized as a physical giant, Paine was assigned the murder of Secretary of State William Seward by Booth. After a determined effort in which he critically wounded five people, he escaped into unknown parts of the city - believed by many to be Congressional Cemetery. Three days later he appeared at the door of Mary Surratt where he and the rest of the household were arrested.

Samuel Bland Arnold. Arnold, together with Michael O'Laughlen, Samuel A. Mudd and Edman Spangler, escaped the gallows only to be sentenced to prison terms. He was pardoned three and a half years later by President Johnson. Arnold survived until 1906, and authored one of the rarer collectibles on the Lincoln assassination entitled, *Confessions of a Lincoln Conspirator.*

the District and Soldiers Home near the then outskirts of the City (current day Florida Avenue). Lincoln had accepted an invitation to attend a special performance by a local group of actors for the convalescing soldiers. At the last minute, however, he cancelled, and instead attended a special ceremony where the members of the 140th Indiana Volunteers presented Governor Oliver P. Morton of Indiana and Lincoln with a captured Confederate battle flag. The two politicians met the regiment in front of the National Hotel and accepted the presentation with the usual political speeches. This last minute rescheduling proved fatal in the long run for while it averted Lincoln's possible kidnapping, it resulted in Booth's decision to roll over the kidnapping plot to one of murder. John Surratt, one of the principals in the kidnapping plot, hid the weapons which Davy Herold had taken to Surrattsville in anticipation of the successful kidnapping of the President. Surratt hid the carbines in the ceiling joists above the dining room of the tavern.

Whatever the plots and whatever the true reasons for meeting, John Lloyd's testimony concerning Mary Surratt's statement to have the *shooting irons* ready was lethal to her. If Lloyd lied to protect himself from the gallows, he showed clever foresight. If he perjured himself he did it without the help of Secretary of War, Edwin Stanton. Lloyd told his story before he was placed under arrest and before he was brought back to Old Capitol Prison in the District. On Tuesday, April 18, just one day after Mary Surratt's arrest, Lloyd was arrested by Lieutenant Alexander Lovett and Captain William Williams of Provost Marshal James O 'Beirne's staff. Lovett and Williams took the innkeeper into custody at Surrattsville. While under cross-examination at the tavern, Lloyd told of the events of Friday, April 14, including the midnight visit of Booth and Herold. In doing so he clearly put a noose around Mary Surratt's neck. Supporters of Mary Surratt are quick to point to Lloyd's history of drinking and his inebriation on the night of the 14th. Besotted or not, Lloyd's testimony was repeated several times; it was unwavering and it stuck. The fact that Louis Weichmann independently corroborated many of the details of Lloyd's testimony did not help Mrs. Surratt's case. The most serious charge that can be leveled against both Weichmann and Lloyd is that they turned state's evidence to save their own necks. While this may have some validity to it, the immunization of witnesses to secure crucial testimony about a crime is a long held practice in jurisprudence and in no way negates the testimony they produce. To the contrary, it more often than not results in a successful conviction. The defense was never able to show that these two key witnesses lied nor were they able to show any contradictions in the testimony. If Weichmann and Lloyd are guilty of anything, it would be saving their own necks and that they did quite effectively.

Arriving a few minutes after midnight, Booth and Herold pulled their sweating mounts up to the door of Lloyd's tavern. Herold dismounted and pounded on the door arousing the sleeping Lloyd. Lloyd had been drinking and was heavily under the influence. Whether he was drunk or not isn't clear. What is clear is that he knew what was happening and responded accordingly. Herold told the dazed innkeeper to get *those things* and to hurry. Lloyd didn't need any additional explanation. When he returned with the two carbines Booth refused his saying that he could not carry it with his injured leg hurting so. Herold took one of the carbines, fashioned a sling for it and told Lloyd to keep the other. Lloyd hid this carbine between the studs of the dining room wall by suspending it from a rope. After downing several swills of whiskey, Booth told Lloyd what they had done. The two fugitives then swiftly turned their mounts and headed south for the small crossroad village known as T. B. a few miles from the Surratt tavern. T.B. presumably took its name from a prominent land owner in the area , Thomas Brooke.

In T. B. stood a tavern operated by a man named John Thompson. It was to this tavern that Davy Herold had come a month earlier, on March 17, after the failure of his cohorts to show up at the Surratt Tavern with the kidnapped President. Herold spent the night of the 17th at Thompson's Tavern. The next morning he met John Surratt and George Atzerodt on the road leading from Thompson's Tavern as he headed back to the Surratt Tavern. Herold had been assigned the job of meeting the kidnappers following their abduction of Lincoln and having the carbines and other items ready for the escape through Maryland into Virginia. These were the items that John Surratt took back to the Surratt Tavern and secreted away between the joists over the dining room and later were brought out by John Lloyd on the night of the 14th for Booth and Herold presumably at the instruction of Mary Surratt.

The two men arrived at T. B. sometime between 1:00 a.m. and 2:00 a.m. where they paused momentarily and then turned from their southerly direction and headed east directly for the home of Dr. Samuel A. Mudd.

According to the statements given by Dr. Mudd prior to and after his arrest, two strangers arrived at his door around 4:00 a.m. on the morning of Saturday, April 15th. Fearing possible harm from renegade or guerilla-type persons roaming the neighborhood, Mudd claims to have proceeded with caution. On becoming convinced that one of the

The restored farmhouse of Dr. Samuel A. Mudd. The architectural appearance is identical to that which Booth and Herold saw when they arrived on the morning of April 15, 1865.

strangers needed medical attention because of a broken leg, Mudd admitted the two men to his house. He attended to the man with the broken leg and prepared a splint for him from the pasteboard sides of a hat box. During the next several hours, the two men were given certain hospitalities of the house and the injured man fed and put to bed. At mid-morning, Dr. Mudd traveled into Bryantown claiming that he had to do a little shopping. The village of Bryantown lay approximately four miles due south of the Mudd farm and consisted of a tavern, store and several houses.

On reaching the village, Mudd was startled to find a troop of Union soldiers, members of the 13th New York Cavalry under Lieutenant David Dana. This was the cavalry that had been sent out around 2:00 a.m. by General Augur as a result of stableman John Fletcher's revelations back in Washington. By mid-morning the soldiers had arrived at the small village of Bryantown and commandeering the local tavern, set up a headquarters. On inquiring, Mudd was shocked to learn that the President had been shot by an assassin the night before and had died at 7:22 a.m. this very day. Mudd further learned from the soldiers that the assassin was the famous actor, John Wilkes Booth. If Mudd had known that the crippled *stranger* at his house was John Wilkes Booth, he would have

Tobacco barn at the Mudd farm. Mudd maintained a limited medical practice while he grew tobacco at his farm in 1865. The Mudd family still grows tobacco on the surrounding acreage as evidenced by the tobacco drying in one of the Mudd barns.

been obligated to inform the soldiers of the suspects whereabouts. Mudd next claims to have continued his errands in Bryantown after which he returned home to his farm. Arriving around 5:00 p.m., Mudd claims to have found the injured man riding away from his house (some 75 yards distant) with his young companion ready to follow. The young man asked Dr. Mudd the directions to a Parson Wilmer's house which lay southwest of Mudd's house across the Zekiah Swamp. After Mudd told him the way, the man rode after his injured friend, and the two disappeared into the distance. Dr. Mudd returned to his wife and went on about his usual business unaware of the grief which lay ahead as a result of his having rendered medical help to the injured stranger, a man he steadfastly claimed not to have known and to have never seen before or since.

Most historians have concluded that the role of Dr. Mudd was no more than that of an innocent physician who became a victim of circumstances at the hands of a vengeful government. Several Presidents from Franklin Roosevelt to Jimmy Carter have been petitioned repeatedly to pardon the convicted doctor as an innocent man. For us to believe, however, that Mudd's greatest sin was his faithful administration of the Hippocratic oath during the early

Dr. Samuel Alexander Mudd. 1833 - 1883.

In 1877 Samuel Cox, Jr. would write that Mudd had confided to him that he knew who Booth was when he visited on Saturday, April 15, and that on learning that Booth was the assassin of President Lincoln, asked him to leave his home immediately rather than inform the soldiers in Bryantown of his presence in the Mudd home.

The tombstone on Dr. Mudd's grave in St. Mary's cemetery located near Bryantown. In this cemetery is also buried Dr. William Queen who arranged the initial meeting between Mudd and Booth.

morning hours of April 15th belies the evidence. Perhaps the failure of each President to pardon Mudd reflected some doubt from other more wise advisors.

When Booth and Herold headed down the road from T. B. toward Dr. Mudd's farm was their visit to the doctor that fateful morning an accident of history, or did they know exactly where they were going and what to expect? Did Booth require medical attention at the moment and did he know that a doctor lived in the vicinity? Clearly, on leaving the Surratt House, the two fugitives altered their direction from due south to southeast and placed the notorious Zekiah Swamp between themselves and the Potomac river crossing.

Consider the following facts for which records exist. In mid-October of 1864, Booth traveled from Montreal, Canada, where he presumably conversed with agents of the Confederate government, to the area around Bryantown. He carried with him a letter of introduction to individuals in the area from a prominent Baltimore merchant and known Confederate agent named Patrick Martin. Booth presented his letter of introduction to Dr. William Queen, another prominent physician and member of the Confederate secret service in southern Maryland. Queen passed Booth and his letter to his son-in-law John Chandler Thompson (not the owner of the tavern in T.B.), who introduced Booth to Samuel Mudd at Saint Mary's Church on Sunday morning, November 12, 1864. Booth spent Monday night, November 13, as Mudd's house guest and the following day, Tuesday, November 14, purchased a horse from Mudd's next door neighbor, George Gardiner. This horse was somewhat unique in that it had lost an eye. It would later be ridden by Lewis Powell on the night of April 14 and it would show up at General Augur's headquarters in the early morning hours following the assassination. A month later, on December 18th, Booth again visited the Bryantown area to attend a meeting at which he was introduced to Thomas Harbin, the chief Confederate Signal Service operative in southern Maryland (the Signal Service was the branch which contained the Confederate Secret Service). This meeting was arranged, according to Thomas Harbin's testimony some years later, at the insistence Dr. Mudd. At this meeting, Harbin claims that Booth enlisted his help in laying out an abduction escape route across the Potomac and into the northern neck of Virginia. Four days after this meeting on December 22, Booth returned to his room at the National Hotel in Washington and on the following day, December 23rd, met with Dr. Mudd for the purpose of yet another introduction to a possible ally, John H. Surratt, Jr. Quite by accident, Mudd and Booth met Surratt and Louis Weichmann on Pennsylvania Avenue while the two were presumably headed for the Surratt boarding house. The four men went to Booth's room in the National Hotel where a conversation took place which figured prominently in the conspiracy trial. While it is difficult to prove exactly what was discussed, the outcome of this meeting according to John Surratt himself, was his enlistment as a member of the kidnapping conspiracy and Mudd's roll was vital in bringing Booth and Surratt together on this particular day.

It was always Mudd's contention that he did not know the stranger who came to his door early on that Saturday morning following the assassination seeking medical help. When confronted by the authorities with certain of the facts mentioned above, Mudd contended that the stranger disguised himself with a false beard and kept a shawl wrapped high around his neck, thus fooling the doctor into recognizing who it really was. Is it possible that Dr. Mudd failed to recognize the stranger who met with him on several other occasions a few months earlier and who had been an overnight guest in his home? Consider the circumstances which Mudd found himself in at the time of his interrogation.

If Mudd had admitted that he recognized his injured visitor as John Wilkes Booth, he clearly would have placed himself in serious jeopardy as a conspirator or as an accomplice of the man who murdered the President. Mudd could not escape the fact that he knew on

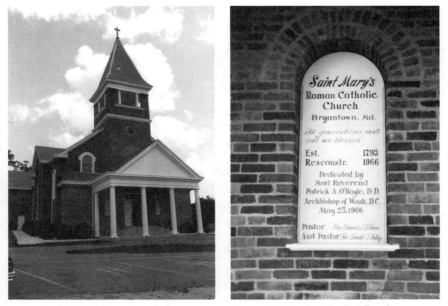

Saint Mary's Church, Bryantown. It was at this church that Booth was introduced to Dr. Mudd which resulted in Booth's spending the night at Mudd's farmhouse. Mudd and his wife are buried in the cemetery which surrounds the church.

Bryantown Tavern. It was here that Mudd arranged a meeting between Booth and Thomas Harbin in December of 1864. It was also at this tavern that the 13th New York Cavalry set up its headquarters on Saturday, April 15.

Saturday noon after talking with the soldiers in Bryantown that John Wilkes Booth had murdered the President. Mudd would have had to inform the soldiers of Booth's presence at his home at that very moment or face being an accessory by harboring the suspect to the assassin's terrible crime. When faced with the situation of hosting the President's assassin or an injured guest, Mudd opted for the latter. He had no choice. Better a doctor should host an injured patient than a suspected killer.

Two additional pieces of information strengthen this view. In later years, after his release from prison, Mudd would confide to another protector of Booth during his attempted escape, Samuel Cox, Jr., that he indeed knew the injured stranger that came to his house in the early morning hours of April 15 to be John Wilkes Booth, but that he had no idea of his crime when first approached in those dawn hours. According to Cox, when Mudd became aware of Booth's mad act while he was in Bryantown passing Confederate mail, he returned home and confronted Booth. Booth admitted his act and pleaded with his accuser "for the sake of his mother." Whatever action Mudd might have contemplated taking at that moment, his final decision was to

Thomas Harbin. Harbin, along with Thomas Jones, served as the principal Confederate secret service operatives along the Potomac River between Southern Maryland and Northern Virginia. Harbin served as postmaster at Piscataway, Maryland. Photo: Surratt Society Museum.

Harbin's post office still stands as the left hand structure of this current residence in Piscataway, Maryland.

William E. Doster. Military counsel appointed to defend Paine and Atzerodt, Doster had served as Provost Marshal for the District in 1864. He kept Atzerodt's statement secretly among his papers. It was finally discovered by Joan Chaconas in the 1970's. From the files of James O. Hall.

tell Booth and Herold to leave immediately and never darken his door again. Perhaps equally damaging to Dr. Mudd's claim of innocence is the statement of Dr. Richard Stewart of Cleydael, yet another person who aided Booth, who later testified that Herold had told him that, *Dr. Mudd had recommended him to me.*

A final piece of incriminating evidence which belies Mudd's protestations of guilt is found in a recently discovered statement given by George Atzerodt shortly after his arrest in Germantown, Maryland. Following his incarceration aboard the monitor *Saugus*, Atzerodt had been visited by the Marshal of Baltimore, James McPhail, at the request of Atzerodt's brother-in-law, John Smith, who served on McPhail's staff. McPhail carefully wrote down the statement which Atzerodt gave him that night and curiously turned the document over to Atzerodt's attorney, William Doster, and not to any of the government's officials. The document apparently remained carefully tucked away with Doster's papers and did not resurface for over one hundred and ten years. Through the tenacious research efforts and some serendipity of amateur historian, Joan L. Chaconas, the statement was finally brought to light. Included in Atzerodt's rambling statement is the clear implication of Samuel Mudd in the conspiracy to abduct Lincoln. Atzerodt states that Mudd knew of the plot and that supplies and food were sent on to his house to be picked up there during the planned escape through Southern Maryland.

The record of Mudd's involvement with Confederate agents in Southern Maryland and his meeting with Booth in November and again in December of 1864 point to his knowledge and complicity in the abortive abduction attempts of early 1865. The statements of Samuel Cox, Jr., Richard Stewart, and George Atzerodt add a heavy weight to the scales of Mudd's complicity. It seems clear that Mudd had become involved in an intolerable situation. He would never have knowingly taken part in the murder of the President no matter how profound his dislike of him or the Union. The law, however, is clear and unforgiving in its requirements of any person who has knowledge of or willingly participates in a conspiracy to commit a crime, even if the individual divests himself of any participation in the conspiracy. No matter how hard he tried, Mudd could not wash Lincoln's blood from his own hands. As latter day apologists for the doctor learn more and more about the irrefutable evidence pointing to Mudd's complicity, they are faced with having to rationalize the meaning of the complicity. In any event, it no longer seems tenable to shield Mudd with the Hippocratic Oath.

Leaving Mudd's house sometime between 5:00 p.m. and 6:00 p.m., Booth and Herold seemed to head west disappearing along the murky

RICH HILL

MID-18TH CENTURY FARM HOUSE (WITH ALTERATIONS AFTER 1800) WAS HOME OF COL. SAMUEL COX. THIS SOUTHERN SYMPATHIZER FED AND SHELTERED FUGITIVES JOHN WILKES BOOTH AND DAVID E. HEROLD BEFORE DAWN ON EASTER SUNDAY, APRIL 16, 1865, FOLLOWING BOOTH'S ASSASSINATION OF PRESIDENT ABRAHAM LINCOLN. BOOTH AND HEROLD HID IN WOODS UNTIL NIGHT OF APRIL 21, WHEN COX'S FOSTER BROTHER, THOMAS A. JONES, HELPED THEM ESCAPE ACROSS THE POTOMAC TO VIRGINIA.

MARYLAND HISTORICAL SOCIETY

Samuel Cox, Sr. Known locally as the Colonel, Cox was a prominent local Confederate sympathizer who secreted Booth and Herold in a thicket near his property. He directed Thomas Jones to care for the two fugitives and see them safely across the river. Photo: Surratt House Museum.

Samuel Cox, Jr. Nineteen years old, Cox was the adopted son of the Colonel. He left an annotated record in a book written by Thomas Jones of a conversation he had with Dr. Mudd in 1878 in which Mudd acknowledged knowing Booth and that he had murdered Lincoln. Photo: Surratt House Museum.

edges of the great Zekiah Swamp. Exactly where or how they ventured for the next three hours is unclear, but at 9:00 p.m. they showed up at the cabin of a man named Oswell Swann some miles southeast of Mudd's farm. Swann was a free black who owned a modest farm whose mortgage had been provided by Samuel Mudd's cousin George Mudd, *a good Union man,* near Hughsville, Maryland which lay *southeast* of Dr. Mudd's and on the east side of the Zekiah swamp. If the two had originally left Mudd's headed west, they reversed themselves at some point and headed southeast. Again, Mudd's testimony to the soldiers comes into question. It seems clear that Booth's next objective was the home of Colonel Samuel Cox known as Rich Hill. Cox's home was situated just west of the Zekiah swamp near the present village of Bel Alton which lay approximately fifteen miles southwest of Bryantown.

In leaving Dr. Mudd's home, it also seems clear that Booth and Herold made a wide circle to the *east* averting the area around Bryantown rather than traveling west as indicated by Mudd. This is evident by their meeting Oswell Swann at his cabin near Hughsville. One can conjecture that Booth and Herold knew that Union troops occupied Bryantown and it would prove lethal for them to venture due south passing through or near the enemy's nest. How the two found out about the soldiers in Bryantown is conjecture, but the good doctor looms large again.

To reach the Colonel's home at Rich Hill required that the two fugitives pass through the swamp, a difficult task which required considerable knowledge of the terrain. Booth and Herold would need the help of an experienced guide. Oswell Swann, well known to Mudd, turned out to be just such a person.

It was near midnight when Swann lead the two saddle weary men up to Cox's front door at Rich Hill. It took the three men just over three hours to navigate the great swamp and emerge on the western side. According to Swann's testimony, the two men were invited into Cox's home where they visited for three or four hours. Cox extended the hospitality of his house to the two fugitives supplying them with food and water. Cox, however, later denied that the two had ever entered his house and he was supported by testimony from one of his servant women, his former slave freed by the dastardly Lincoln, who said that the two strangers had remained outside on horseback. Oswell Swann's testimony contradicted Cox's and his servants. Swann's testimony would appear to be the more believable in that he had nothing to protect by perjuring himself while the servant did. It only seems reasonable that the two fugitives would rest with the Confederate agent after their harrowing passage through the swamp.

Huckleberry, the home of Thomas A. Jones is today a part of Loyola, a Jesuit retreat on the Potomac. Jones briefly stopped here to get Booth and Herold food as he led them down to the Potomac on the night of April 20.

It is clear that Cox knew exactly who his two visitors were that Sunday morning as he made arrangements with his foreman, Franklin Robey, to secret them in a pine thicket some two miles from his house.

The following morning Cox sent his adopted son, Samuel Cox, Jr., to get Thomas A. Jones, a Confederate operative who lived a short distance from the Potomac River. Jones came at once to see what Cox wanted and was told by the Colonel that he had Booth and Herold hidden in a thicket and wanted Jones to care for them. This care included getting them over the river into Virginia. Jones, who claimed a strong loyalty to the Colonel, agreed to do whatever asked. For the next five days he diligently cared for the two fugitives bringing them food, drink and newspapers, the latter of which Booth intently read and reread. These five days were perhaps the grimmest of Booth's life. Forced to live outdoors with little protection from the elements; cold, hungry and anxious to move on to safer and more hospitable surroundings, Booth was at his lowest point of the past several days.

Jones had been prevented from sending his contraband across the river because of the increasing activity of the military throughout the area. Finally, on Thursday, April 20, Jones came to the two men and advised them that he would send them over the river that evening. Jones later wrote that he had been forced to abort earlier attempts

A short distance from this marker is the site of the thicket where Jones hid Booth and Herold for four days before sending them across the Potomac.

Years later Thomas Jones told his story of hiding Booth and Herold in the Pine thicket. He later identified the locality of the thicket as being opposite the home of *Mr. Collis* which was built right after the war. Historian James O. Hall discovered the original Collis house incorporated into the house now standing on the site.

because of the intense troop activity in the area. On April 20, while visiting a tavern in Port Tobacco, Jones overheard a group of soldiers discussing a false report that Booth and Herold had been seen attempting to cross the river at a point much further south. Jones quickly realized that the troops would be off on a wild goose chase and he would have a narrow window of opportunity in which to get his fugitives across the river. Jones, according to his later writings, came for the two men in the late hours of the evening and under the protection of darkness led them from their hiding place in the thicket toward the river; the last barrier to Virginia. Jones placed Booth on one of his horses while he and Herold walked on foot. After a short while they came to Jones' home, named *Huckleberry* where Booth and Herold waited outside while Jones went in to get both food and drink for his *friends*.

After leaving *Huckleberry*, the three made their way a short mile to the bluff overlooking the Potomac River. Here Booth dismounted and with the help of Jones and Herold, made his way down the slope to the rivers edge. Jones had a small skiff hidden in a small creek which flowed through the ravine emptying into the Potomac. Pulling the boat from the creek, Jones motioned the two to get in. Booth

The small creek where Jones hid the skiff which he gave to Booth to use in crossing the river. This creek flows into the Potomac after passing through Dent's Meadow.

44

The home of Mrs. Elizabeth Quesenberry located on Machodoc Creek. The original *cottage* of Mrs. Quesenberry was only the left portion of this modern home.

sat in the stern with a sculling oar while Davy Herold pulled at the oars. With the aid of a small candle provided by Jones and Booth's wood-boxed compass, the two men set out for the far Virginia shore near Mathias Point.

It was while Booth was hiding in the pine thicket that he finally had time to read the papers which Jones had supplied and see what the world thought of him and his act. What he read dismayed him. Far from being cast as Brutus or William Tell, both liberators of despots, Booth was characterized as a *common cutthroat* with *every mans hand against me*. Did Booth really believe the country would look upon him as a liberator removing the most hated tyrant in our country's history? *I struck for my country, and her alone,* he wrote. *A people ground beneath this tyranny prayed for the end, and yet see how the cold hands they extend me!*

If Booth looked upon his act as one which freed an oppressed people from a tyrant, he had reason to believe it true. Lincoln had been villified by much of the press of the day, South and North, as a tyrant who had usurped certain inalienable rights including the privilege of habeas corpus. Northern military prisons were full of persons arrested without charge, tried without benefit of the civil courts, and sentenced by military tribunal. At times Lincoln seemed to pursue the bloodiest war in history with a determined passion that was exceeded by no one including the abolitionists who had started it in the first place. The calls for Lincoln's head were continuous from the day of his election until the day of his death. The War for the Union had become, at times, a war of slow attrition; attrition that drained the South of its resources and the North of its will. By the early summer of 1864, the Republican party had all but given up on its leader and movements were afoot to dump Lincoln as the party candidate in favor of someone who could win. The problem was that winning the election would be at the expense of winning the war. Lincoln knew this and even privately conceded the unlikelihood of his reelection. In a carefully penned note he wrote to his cabinet which he planned to reveal to them only after the election, Lincoln had acknowledged the likelihood of his upcoming defeat. In his predicted defeat, he lamented for the Union which he claimed would be the victim of his opponents election victory. Peace at any price is not new to the American political scene. Prosecution of the war was, at times, more difficult for Lincoln in the North than it was for him against the South. Lincoln did not represent a united front with the people of the North and many wished him gone, even dead. Among his efforts to secure reelection, he even found it necessary to abandon the new Republican Party for a coalition party named The

Cleydael, the summer home of Dr. Richard Stuart. Booth and Herold arrived here at dusk on Sunday evening, April 23.

National Union Party. If Jefferson Davis was the *beau ideal* of the southern people and the southern cause, he reflected their feelings when he wrote shortly after being told of Lincoln's murder, *we could not be expected to mourn his death.* God's will be done!

John J. Hughes. After Jones pushed Booth and Herold into the Potomac on the night of April 20, the two eventually wound up back on the Maryland side of the river where they were cared for by John J. Hughes. Photo: Surratt House Museum.

Mathias Point, Virginia. Thomas Jones had told Booth and Herold to head for Mathias Point directly opposite their launch point on the Maryland side of the river. After their delay at Nanjemoy, they finally crossed to Mathias Point.

VIRGINIA - AT LAST!

Once out into the Potomac river, things began to go wrong for the two fugitives. Either the incoming tide or the threat of cruising gunboats forced Booth and Herold off their course and further upriver. Missing their target, Mathias Point on the Virginia side, the two apparently hit Blossom Point on the Maryland side and carefully made their way up Nanjemoy Creek. Here they worked their way to the farm of Peregrin Davis, who like everyone else throughout this region (except George Mudd), was a strong Confederate supporter. Apparently, Herold knew exactly where to go after recognizing they had entered Nanjemoy Creek. Here Davis' son-in-law, John J. Hughes, provided food and whatever else the two men needed. Resting from their abortive attempt to cross the river on Thursday evening and Friday morning, the pair remained hidden near the Davis' farm all day Saturday and did not attempt a second crossing until Saturday night again under the protective cover of darkness. This time the two were successful. Reaching Mathias Point on the Virginia side, they made their way along the shore until they reached a small creek a short distance south named *Gambo Creek*. According to Davy Herold's later testimony, he and Booth had been told to head for *Machodoc Creek* just south of Mathias Point. At first the pair mistook Gambo Creek for their ultimate destination but soon recovered their bearings and made their way southward along the shore toward the next creek which emptied into the Potomac, Machodoc. It was near the mouth of Machodoc Creek that Mrs. Elizabeth Quesenberry lived. The gentle Mrs. Quesenberry was well plugged into the Confederate spy network that ran across and along the river and northern Virginia. Booth was made aware of Mrs. Quesenberry by Thomas Jones who had told him that she would put him in the hands of a man named Thomas Harbin. Now Booth's connection with this chief Confederate agent back in November of 1864 at the Bryantown Tavern would pay off. Thanks to Samuel Mudd and his arranged meeting between Booth and Harbin, Booth would soon be in helping hands. Originally brought in to the kidnapping plot by Booth at the Bryantown meeting, Harbin was to help run Lincoln over the river and through northern Virginia. Now Harbin found himself with an assassin and his accomplice who needed his help in a different way.

Elizabeth Quesenberry quickly sent word for Harbin to come to her house as soon as possible. Sometime during the early afternoon

Harbin arrived at the Quesenberry home with one of his Confederate operatives in tow, a man named Joseph Baden. The two confederate operatives took Booth and Herold a short distance to the home of another agent named William Bryant. The two men were placed in the care of Bryant who supplied them with horses and agreed to pass them on to yet another member of the Confederate underground which ran through southern Maryland and northern Virginia, Dr. Richard Stewart. Stewart owned a large frame house some distance south of Machodoc Creek and a few miles inland from the Potomac. The home served as his summer retreat which he called *Cleydael*. Stewart lived most of the year in a spacious Georgian mansion just south of Washington on the Virginia shore of the Potomac which he called Cedar Grove. Cleydael, a less pretentious home than Cedar Grove, was located some eight miles south of the river in a remote area of King George County. Stewart had run afoul of the Federal authorities as a suspected runner of supplies needed by the Confederacy and had only recently been released from Old Capitol Prison. When Bryant arrived Sunday night at Cleydael with his two fugitives, he found a somewhat inhospitable Stewart. Closely associated with the Confederate underground, Stewart in all probability knew who his uninvited guests were and wanted no part of them. Refusing to provide shelter or medical attention, Stewart reluctantly agreed to allow the two scruffs to come into his kitchen to eat, but only after considerable argument and

The ferry slip at Port Royal as it appeared in the early 1900's.
The site is still used as a boat ramp today.

hesitation. After permitting this small grace, Stewart sent Bryant and his two companions a short distance away to the log cabin of William Lucas, a free black who made a modest living farming.

Here lies an interesting twist in the saga. Insulted by the treatment he had received from Stewart, from whom he fully expected help as a southern partisan, Booth felt obliged to repay the doctor in kind for his lack of hospitality. Booth decided to send Stewart a penciled note written on one of the pages which he tore from his little memorandum book which he kept as a diary, and a small amount of money to pay for the meager food he and Herold had been proffered. In this way, Booth had intended to insult the southern gentleman for his lack of grace in hosting his guests. Stewart's inhospitality and Booth's reaction to it, probably saved the doctor's neck. In his note, Booth insulted Stewart by offering to pay for the food - a definite affront to a Virginia gentleman, and emphasized his pointed anger at the doctor by scribbling a quote from Macbeth, *The sauce in meat is ceremony. Meeting were bare without it.* Booth's point was that although Stewart finally offered the two wretched souls food, the manner of the offer was as important as the offer itself and the doctor had failed in his lack of southern graciousness in proffering help. Later, when questioned by the authorities, Booth's insulting note would support the doctor's claim that he had not befriended the fugitives.

Map showing the relationship of Port Conway to Port Royal on the Rappahannock River.

The Sauce in Meat is Ceremony

The following text is taken from a note penned by John Wilkes Booth and given to Dr. Richard Stewart by Charlie Lucas at the direction of Booth. Following what Booth thought was inhospitable treatment unbecoming a southern gentleman, particularly a Confederate agent, Booth felt obliged to upbraid the doctor for his rudeness. He at first wrote a note which mentioned five dollars, but changing his mind, decided to give the doctor only two dollars and a half and wrote a second note. The first note was recovered with Booth's memorandum book (diary) while the second note was recovered from Stewart. The notes were presented by the prosecution at Andrew Johnson's impeachment trial in 1867 and recorded as evidence, but have since disappeared. Booth decided to dramatizes his anger at Stewart with a quote from Macbeth, Act III, scene 4 (bold typeface).

Dear Sir: Forgive me, but I have some little pride. I hate to blame you for your want of hospitality; you know your own affairs. I was sick and tired, with a broken leg, in need of medical advice. I would not have turned a dog from my door in such a condition. However, you were kind enough to give me something to eat, for which I not only thank you, but on account of the reluctant manner in which it was bestowed, I feel bound to pay for it. It is not the substance, but the manner in which a kindness is extended that makes one happy in the acceptance thereof. **The sauce in meat is ceremony; meeting were bare without it.** *Be kind enough to accept the enclosed two dollars and a half (though hard to spare) for what we have received.*

yours, respectfully,
Stranger

April 24, 1865
To Dr. Stewart

Booth's note to Dr. Richard Stewart. The original was last seen at the impeachment trial of Andrew Johnson in 1867.

Arriving at William Lucas' cabin in the early hours of Monday morning, April 24, Booth and Herold were in no mood to negotiate with a black man. The elderly Lucas and his wife were rudely evicted from their small cabin with intimations of violence. The two men then spent the rest of the early morning hours inside.

When dawn finally came, Booth and Herold tried to persuade Lucas to carry them to the next point along their escape trail - the small village of Port Conway on the Rappahannock River. Lucas declined until Booth threatened violence by drawing his revolver and pointing it at the elder Lucas. Lucas then volunteered his 21 year old son Charley and his wagon for which Booth graciously paid the man $20.00. The younger Lucas then drove the two fugitives ten miles southeast to the village of Port Conway situated on the banks of the Rappahannock River.

After traveling for approximately two hours the three men arrived at the home of William Rollins situated along the northern shore of the Rappahannock River in Port Conway. Herold and Booth tried to get Rollins to take them across the river but were unable to come to any final arrangement. The ferry, which ran the river, was owned by a man named Champe Thornton who lived on the far side of the river in the village of Port Royal. While Booth and Herold waited impatiently for the ferry to return to Port Conway to pick them up, three Confederate soldiers rode up to the ferry slip. They were Lieutenant Mortimer B. Ruggles, and Privates Absalom Bainbridge and Willie Jett. The three were members of Colonel John S. Mosby's famous command and were returning to their homes following the disbanding of Mosby's command the previous week. At first Herold, who did all of the talking, represented himself and Booth as two brothers with the last name of Boyd. Booth was identified as James W. Boyd (J.W.B.). At some point during their conversation, Herold told the soldiers his and Booth's real names and that they were the assassins of Lincoln. With this knowledge the three Confederates, nonetheless, agreed to take the two fugitives with them over the river and help them find refuge. Sometime around noon, James Thornton, a free black who operated the ferry for Champe Thornton, came across the river and took the five men and three horses over to the Port Royal side. Historian James O. Hall points out that William Rollins' young bride, Betsy Rollins, made an observation about the five men that would be crucial to the military authorities later in eventually cornering the two fugitives.

After docking at the ferry slip on the southern bank of the Rappahannock, the five men, riding two to a horse, rode up the small incline from the river bank which ran past the home of Randolph

Arriving in Port Royal, Private Willie Jett first tried to find Booth and Herold lodging at the home of Randolph Peyton who was not at home. His two sisters, Lucy and Sarah Jane were, however, and after first agreeing, decided that it would not be proper for the two men to spend the night while the man of the house was away.

Peyton, a respectable frame house a few hundred feet from the ferry slip. At home on this Monday afternoon were Peyton's two spinster sisters, Lucy and Sarah Jane. Randolph Peyton was away on business. Young Willie Jett, who was well known by the sisters, asked if the wounded confederate and his friend could spend the night. After some discussion which surely included an appeal to patriotism, the sisters decided that it would not be proper for two strangers to spend the night while the man of the house was absent. Undoubtedly, the disheveled appearance of the two men did little to instill patriotic fervor in the spinster sisters. Young Jett graciously backed off and thanked the ladies for their time.

The five men then headed on down the road toward Bowling Green, approximately ten miles south of the river crossing. Four miles south of Port Royal, the travelers turned into the road leading up to the home of Mr. Richard Garrett. Here the affable Willie Jett asked Mr. Garrett to let the injured man, who he introduced as James W. Boyd, stay and rest before continuing on. Jett would return later for Mr. Boyd. Garrett, less concerned about appearances and more inclined toward patriotism, agreed and gave Booth the hospitality of his house while Herold and the three soldiers doffed their caps and continued on to Bowling Green.

Midway between Garrett's and Bowling Green stood the establishment of a woman named Martha Carter. Mrs. Carter, together with her four daughters, lived in a small frame house along the road between the two villages where they frequently provided entertainment for any and all who sought such forms of pleasure. The four men decided to stop at Mrs. Carter's house during the early evening and presumably enjoyed the entertainment of the young Carter girls.

About dark, Bainbridge, Ruggles, Jett and Herold then continued on to Bowling Green where they stopped at the Star Hotel, a hostelry operated by a man named Gouldman. Mr. Gouldman had an attractive young daughter name Izora who Willie Jett had been courting. It was no secret to most of the locals and young Betsy Rollins was well plugged in to the local gossip. It was decided that while Jett and Ruggles would spend the night at the Gouldman's Star Hotel, Herold and Bainbridge would go on to the home of a man named Joseph Clarke, a short distance south of Bowling Green. Clarke had served with Bainbridge in the Confederate army and was a friend of his. And so the four men split up as the last of Monday faded away. To the north, John Wilkes Booth alias James W. Boyd was sound asleep, resting more peacefully than he had for the past several days, now among hospitable people who would not think of turning a southern soldier out into the cold night. April 24th ended on a high note for the two fugitives as things finally began to look up.

Tuesday morning dawned bright as Bainbridge and Herold returned to Bowling Green after a night at the Clarke house to pick up

Site of the old *Star Hotel* in Bowling Green where Willie Jett courted the owner's daughter, Izora Gouldman. Jett was arrested here in the early hours of April 26.

The Garrett farmhouse as it appeared in the mid 1930's shortly before its collapse.

Jett and Ruggles. The four men met exchanging pleasantries after which Bainbridge and Ruggles decided to continue on home. Young Willie Jett, however, would stay on at Gouldman's - he liked the company. The three men soon left Bowling Green and headed north back toward the Garrett farm where John Wilkes Booth was enjoying the pleasant company of Lucinda Hollaway, a teacher boarding with the Garretts, and young Annie Garrett.

On the return trip from Bowling Green to Richard Garretts', the three men again stopped by the home of Mrs. Carter where they *visited* with the entertaining Carter sisters. Having finished their business at Mrs. Carter's, Ruggles, Bainbridge and Herold rode on the seven miles to the Garrett house where they dropped off Herold who joined his resting companion. It was now late Tuesday afternoon.

While proceeding back north, toward Port Royal and Thornton's Ferry, the two soldiers, Bainbridge and Ruggles, were startled to see a troop of yankee cavalry gathering at the ferry slip, apparently ready to ride in the direction of Garrett's farm. The large number of blue coats frightened them, and for reasons known only to Bainbridge and Ruggles, the two Confederates felt it essential to ride back to Garrett's and warn Booth and Herold of the imminent danger they were in.

Returning to Garrett's at dusk, Bainbridge and Ruggles told Booth what they had seen and then headed off in a gallop. Booth, now frightened by the presence of soldiers, wisely scrambled into the surrounding wood with Herold in tow as the Garretts looked on with growing suspicion. Back at the ferry slip, Lieutenant Edward P. Doherty and a troop of twenty six veterans of the 16th New York Cavalry rode out of Port Royal heading due south. How did this contingent of cavalry find themselves so close to their quarry at this moment and how did they get here?

Lucinda Holloway. Lucinda Holloway was the sister of Mrs. Richard Garrett and lived at the Garrett farmhouse. Following Booth's wounding and capture, Lucinda provided a pillow for his head and tried to make him comfortable by offering the dying man water. Dr. Urquhart summoned from nearby Port Royal arrived to proclaim Booth's wound as fatal. Following Booth's death just after daybreak, Dr. Urquhart clipped a lock of Booth's hair from his head and gave it to the young Lucinda Holloway. Today, the lock of hair resides in private hands. Miss Holloway also took Booth's fieldglasses which had been delivered to John Lloyd by Mary Surratt, and sent them to her mother's house where they were later retrieved by Lieutenant Baker and used as evidence in the conspiracy trial. Years later, Lucinda Holloway would write extensively of the events surrounding the capture and death of John Wilkes Booth.

THE CAVALRY ARRIVES

On Monday, April 24, while Booth was resting at the Garrett farm, Stanton's Chief of the Secret Service, Colonel Lafayette C. Baker, paid a visit to the War Department's Telegraph Office. Baker had stopped by to see his old friend Major Thomas Eckert, second in command to Secretary of War Stanton and head of the telegraph office. It was Eckert who Lincoln had approached on the afternoon of April 14 after the Grants had canceled his invitation and invited to join him and Mrs. Lincoln that evening. Eckert declined at the urging of Stanton which has been cited by some as yet another piece of evidence supporting a Stanton conspiracy in Lincoln's murder.

Eckert had just received a telegraphic message from Port Tobacco which erroneously claimed that Booth and Herold had crossed over the Potomac on Sunday, April 16. We know now that Booth and Herold were hiding in the pine thicket where Cox had them taken and that they did not attempt to cross the river until the following Sunday, April 23. In fact, it was actually Thomas Harbin and Joseph Baden who crossed the river on the April 16 presumably to see Mrs. Quesenberry among others. Unfortunately for Booth, it didn't matter. The message which Eckert received from Port Tobacco resulted in an immediate response on Baker's part to set out in the right direction for the wrong reason. Baker, a man who held Stanton's complete confidence and support, immediately went to the Secretary and secured an order from him allowing him a troop of cavalry to pursue Booth and Herold into Virginia. The 16th New York Cavalry provided this troop.

By late evening, Baker had rounded up the necessary men under the command of Lieutenant Edward P. Doherty and added to it his cousin Lieutenant Luther Baker and Lieutenant-Colonel Everton Conger. While Everett Conger was the ranking officer, he quickly passed command on to Lieutenant Doherty. Conger had served in combat and was reassigned to Washington as a result of his having received severe wounds earlier in the war. Conger knew that Doherty was better equipped to handle the contingent of troopers.

Boarding a steamer at the Old Washington Arsenal (currently Fort Lesley McNair), the *John S. Ide*, the soldiers headed down the Potomac River to docks at Belle Plaine, northeast of Port Conway on the Rappahannock. Arriving around 10:00 o'clock in the evening, they began to move southeast questioning people about the possible

Major Thomas Eckert. 1825 - 1910. Assistant Secretary of War under Stanton. On Monday, April 24, while Luther Baker visited him in the War Department Telegraph Office, Eckert received a message which set in motion the final phase of the manhunt for Booth and Herold.

whereabouts of two men, one known to be a cripple. Scouring the countryside as they went, the troop worked its way to Port Conway arriving just after noon on April 25th. Interrogating William Rollins, they learned that two men answering the description of Booth and Herold had ferried the Rappahannock the day before. With them were three Confederate soldiers one of whom was Willie Jett. Mrs. Rollins volunteered her observation to the three officers, an observation that ultimately results in the death of Booth and the capture of Herold. The pretty Betsy Rollins knew that Jett was sweet on the Gouldman girl and, knowing lovers, would in all likelihood be in Bowling Green with his sweetheart. After a short debate amongst the officers as to the best strategy, Doherty concluded that Jett was a sure catch and therefore it was best to go after him and hope to catch the others with him. If they were not with Jett, he would surely be able to tell Doherty where they were. The search party mounted up and headed down the road to Bowling Green.

When Bainbridge and Ruggles approached the ferry in early evening on Tuesday, April 25 and saw the posse of *blue bellies* forming at the ferry, it was Doherty and the 16th New York Cavalry just coming over the river after questioning Rollins and his new bride Betsy.

In tow was William Rollins directing the search party while *under arrest.* The mistaken telegram of the day before and the romantic eye of the storekeepers wife would bring the unlucky Booth to his eventual end.

Now, almost dark, the soldiers rode hard past the farmhouse of Richard Garrett where the fugitives were hiding in the surrounding woods. Seven miles outside of Bowling Green, Doherty pulled up to the Carter House. The Carter girls had never seen so many men in the short period of two days. Business on this visit was more serious than usual, however. As the troop remained on alert outside, Doherty, Baker and Conger entertained the *ladies* with questions. At first, the ladies were of no help and maintained that they had seen no one and knew nothing. Suspicious and using a ruse that only a clever detective would think of, Baker informed the ladies that the crippled man and his companion had actually raped a young girl and were attempting to escape justice. That was enough to loosen up the Carter girls who revealed their visitation by the men the day before. Most importantly, Willie Jett was among them, but there was no lame man with them. This proved puzzling to the officers at first, but they knew they were getting close. Find Jett and Booth had to be near by. Doherty decided to continue on to Bowling Green and Willie Jett.

It was just past midnight when the troop of dirty, saddle-weary veterans rode into Bowling Green and surrounded the Star Hotel. The men had been riding hard for over 24 hours in hostile country. They were short of reason and their adrenalin was flowing as they knew they were closing in on their kill. Dispensing with formalities, Doherty and his men dragged the sleeping Jett from his bed which he shared with Izora Gouldman's brother and shoved a Colt Army .44 to his head. Jett was quickly convinced to talk. He told the impatient soldiers all that he knew. Placed under arrest and tied to his saddle at his own request, Jett agreed to lead the horsemen back up the road to Garrett's farm.

Back at Garrett's, Booth and Herold had returned from their hideout in the woods and were now bedded down in a tobacco barn not far from the house. Either because they feared being trapped in the farm house or because the Garretts no longer trusted the two strangers, Booth and Herold had wound up in the barn instead of the house. The latter was probably the truth for the Garrett boys had placed a padlock on the barn door after the two had bedded down presumably to keep them from stealing any horses and riding off during the night. While they slept, the two Garrett boys, Jack and William hid themselves in a corn crib nearby taking turns to keep an eye on the two suspicious men.

THE CAPTURE

Lieutenant Doherty lead his squad of soldiers up to the farmhouse and motioned them to encircle the building. With the property secure the three officers stamped onto the porch of Garrett's house and banging roughly on the door called for the owner. Richard Garrett, frightened by the rough looking men at his door, opened it slowly. He was quickly pulled outside and a gun shoved in his face. Under the usual questioning by the Yankee trio, Garrett could only stutter - an apparent affliction which became more pronounced because of his fright. Their patience completely gone, the soldiers dragged the old man to a tree where a rope had been tossed over one of the branches. He was challenged to talk or hang. The old man only stuttered harder. At that moment, his son Jack broke the silence and told the officers what they wanted to hear. Locked in the barn were the two men the soldiers were looking for. The troopers quickly surrounded the barn and the unlucky Jack Garrett was told to unlock the door, go in and bring Booth and Herold out. No luck. Booth would not budge. Garrett stumbled out of the barn into Baker's grasp shaking with fright. Luther Baker then tried to talk Booth out, but to no avail. Booth tried to get the soldiers to back off so that he could come out and have a *fighting chance*. Ever the actor, Booth wanted to shoot it out in a final blaze of glory. After further negotiations, Booth told the soldiers that his companion wanted to surrender. Doherty agreed. Herold was quickly grabbed at the door and dragged to a tree a safe distance from the barn where he was tightly bound. It was now obvious that Booth meant to fight it out, to the death if necessary. All thought of returning to Washington to *clear his name* had now vanished.

Doherty finally decided to set the barn on fire in order to flush Booth out. He signaled to his men surrounding the building and several piles of dried pine branches were thrown against a corner of the building. One of the men set them afire. Soon the light from the fire grew bright enough to illuminate the figure of a man inside the barn. Booth was seen leaning on a single crutch with a carbine in one hand and an army Colt in the other. The trapped assassin began to turn about in different directions as if confused as to which way to go. The fire began to blaze rapidly illuminating the entire area. As he turned toward the door of the barn, the crutch dropped from under his arm. At that moment a single shot rang out and the crippled man fell to the floor. Sergeant Boston Corbett, had followed the orders of the Lord and

Booth, after he was shot by Boston Corbett, was dragged from the burning barn and laid on the porch of the Garrett farmhouse.

Placed on the porch of Richard Garrett's house, Booth, paralyzed by the wound, survived for about an hour. He presumably asked that his mother be told that he died for his country.

acted quickly to avenge the Devil's agent.

Mortally wounded, Booth was carried to the porch of the farm house where he was carefully stretched out. Conscious the whole while, Booth would die near dawn on April 26, twelve days after he began his long and painful flight. At this very moment, Abraham Lincoln's body lay in state in the New York City Hall where in three hours the doors would open to 200,000 mourners who had come to see the Civil War President.

Who shot Booth and why? Much speculation has swirled about this crucial act leading some authors to harbor grave suspicions of a sinister conspiracy. Killing Booth, against orders to the contrary, is believed to have been an act secretly ordered by Secretary of War Stanton to silence his *tool* in a monstrous conspiracy to murder Abraham Lincoln. In subsequent years, a series of historians and quasi-historians would weave their intriguing webs of conspiracy fingering a host of master plotters from close members of Lincoln's own cabinet to the Pope himself. Booth's death, however, covered up nothing. It did uncover a series of titillating adventure stories designed to entice the unsuspecting history buff. The best evidence is that Booth was shot by

This special marker is located at the Garrett site. It reads: *Exact northeast corner of the Garrett farmhouse as ascertained by Bob Bergantino. The Garrett farmhouse fell in on itself in the mid 1930's. This stake the courtesy of The Surratt Society. Clinton, Md. H.C. Embrey.*

the man who immediately stepped forward and admitted his act - Boston Corbett. Corbett was a Sergeant in the 16th New York and a battle-hardened veteran who had seen the *elephant* on several occasions during his service. His record was good, and nothing in it would support the contention that he lied to gain some personal glory or that he acted under secret orders from Secretary Stanton. All the evidence to date suggests that he was in the right position at the right time, and he acted from the belief that he was doing exactly what was expected of a soldier facing the enemy. His orders, according to Corbett, had come from God and for that one brief moment, he was the Lord's avenging angel. The fact that Corbett was never punished for what he did in no way lends credence to his act as being privately sanctioned by a hidden conspiracy.

With the death of Booth and the capture of Herold, the most sensational manhunt in our nations history came to an end. Now the second chapter in this grim story was about to unfold. In custody were eight conspirators soon to be charged with the murder of the Chief Executive of the United States. Two were not available to be tried. Booth of course was dead and John H. Surratt, Jr. was missing, believed lost somewhere in the vastness of the country. The truth was that he was in Canada where friends were hiding him from the government manhunt still seeking him out. A long and troublesome trial before a military tribunal was about to begin for the eight now in custody. A trial whose conduct and outcome still continues in controversy to this

Sergeant Boston Corbett of the 16th New York Cavalry stepped forward and freely admitted to shooting Booth in the burning barn at Garrett's. The careful forensic research of Dr. John K. Lattimer of Columbia University supports the claim of Corbett. Despite later accounts of Corbett's mental derangement, he had an excellent military record and was a *fighting* cavalryman.

Mary Elizabeth Surratt. 1823 - 1865.

According to President Andrew Johnson, Mary Surratt *kept the nest that hatched the egg* of the assassination plot. The first woman to be executed by the U.S. Government, she lies buried in Mount Olivet Cemetery in Northeast Washington. Her tavern in Surrattsville is the home of the Surratt Society, a volunteer organization devoted to the preservation and interpretation of the Mary Surratt House and Tavern.

Following release of her body in 1869, Mary Surratt was buried in the Mount Olivet Cemetery in northwest Washington. The original tombstone, now in the museum at the Surratt House in Clinton, Maryland, was replaced with the special marker shown here.

very day.

As Booth's body was being carried back to Washington from the Garrett farm via steamer, untold numbers of men and women shook in the chill of the night in dreaded anticipation of a government dragnet. It would sweep across the countryside along the back roads of Prince Georges and Charles County from Surrattsville to Bryantown, from Port Conway to Bowling Green, a sickening fear gripped dozens who had fed and cared for the crippled stranger and his friend - a fear that came from the anticipated moment when a loud knock would fall against their door and blue-coated messengers would drag them away. Although hundreds were rounded up, in the end all would escape the vengeful reach of a government intent on following Stanton's directive to *remove the stain of innocent blood from the land.*

Of the conspirators brought to trial before a military tribunal, four would hang and four would go to prison. Mary Surratt, Lewis Paine Powell, George Atzerodt and Davy Herold were hanged at the Old Arsenal. Edman Spangler, Michael O'Laughlen, Samuel Arnold and the fortunate Dr. Mudd would be sentenced to varying periods in prison,

To remove the stain of innocent blood from the land.

The following statement is taken from a special War Department circular issued by Secretary of War Edwin McMasters Stanton on April 20, 1865. Ten days later, on May 1, 1865, President Andrew Johnson issued a special Executive Order removing jurisdiction of the conspirators from the civil courts and placing them under the jurisdiction of the military. Interestingly, the original draft of Johnson's order is in the hand of Stanton and appears on War Department letterhead. Is Stanton's Order of April 20 legal? Did the President have the authority to establish a military tribunal and place the accused under its jurisdiction? Stanton's Order of April 20 had ominous implications for many people. Listed below are the names of those individuals who readily fall within the Secretary of War's order, but who were never brought to trial before the military tribunal.

... all persons harboring or secreting the said persons (Booth and Herold) ... or aiding ... their concealment or escape, will be treated as accomplices in the murder of the President ... and shall be subject to trial before a military commission, and the punishment of death.

Official Records, Series I, Volume 46, Section 3.

John M. Lloyd
Oswell Swann
Dr. Richard Stuart
Thomas Jones
Colonel Samuel Cox
Peregrin Davis
John J. Hughes
Franklin Roby
William Lucas
Charlie Lucas

Thomas Harbin
Mrs. Elizabeth Quesenberry
William Bryant
Joseph Baden
Private Willie Jett
Private Mortimer Ruggles
Lieutenant Absalom Bainbridge

all of which would be served out at the Federal Fort known as Fort Jefferson in the Dry Tortugas off the southern tip of Florida. O'Laughlen would die of yellow fever while the remaining three would be pardoned by President Andrew Johnson as one of his last acts before leaving office in 1869 in defiance of the Radical Republicans. Thus the good Dr. Mudd, who had escaped the hangman's noose by only one vote, would serve a little over three years before returning home to his wife and children and a life of denial. He would bring Edman Spangler home with him and provide for him until his death a few years later. The country would attempt to *bind up the nation's wounds* but the scar left by Booth and his accomplices would remain for a century yet to come.

Shortly after 1:30 p.m. on the afternoon of July 7, 1865, the four condemned conspirators were hanged at the Washington Arsenal (now Fort Lesley J. McNair). The scaffold stood just to the right (see below) of the present Quarters 20. From left to right: Mary Surratt, Lewis Paine, David Herold and George A. Atzerodt.

The 541 H Street boarding house (now 604) where several of the conspirators met at various times. It was here on Monday evening, April 17, that Lewis Paine came unexpectedly resulting in Mary Surratt's arrest.

A bogus Mary Surratt. Within hours of Lincoln's death, enterprising entrepreneurs began selling photographs of the various conspirators to a curious public. This photograph was sold to an unsuspecting public as being that of Mary Surratt. It is in the Osborn H. Oldroyd collection of the National Park Service.

Quarters 20 at Fort Lesley J. McNair, the modern day survivor of that part of the old Penitentiary Building where the military trial of the conspirators was held. On the third floor of this building the ghost of Mary Surratt is still believed to walk at midnight.

Major General David Hunter. Hunter served as President of the Military Tribunal which tried the eight conspirators at the Old Washington Arsenal. The legal jurisdiction of the tribunal has been generally accepted by most historians to be without merit.

The *National Hotel* located
on Pennsylvania Avenue at
Sixth Street.   Here Booth
was introduced to John H.
Surratt, Jr. by Dr. Mudd on
December 23, 1864.

Edwin McMasters Stanton.
Booth's real adversary.
Stanton directed nearly every
detail of the manhunt for
Booth during the twelve days
of his flight.   Latter-day
writers would develope the
elaborate theory that
Stanton was behind Lincoln's
murder and had orchestrated
a conspiracy behind the
scenes. There is no evidence,
direct or circumstantial, to
support such a theory.

Soldiers Home. Located approximately three miles due north of the Capitol building, this house served as the summer White House for the Lincolns from 1862 to 1864. Lincoln's hat was shot off one evening as he approached the main gate on horseback. An abduction plot engineered by Brigadier General Bradley T. Johnson of Early's command was scheduled for the summer of 1864 but abandoned by Early prior to his famous raid on Washington.

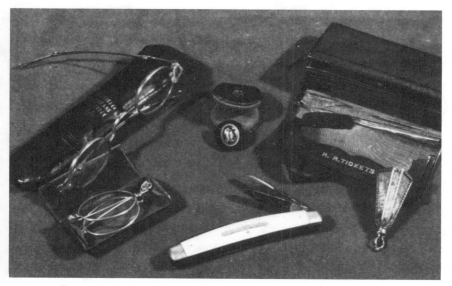

Contents of Lincoln's pockets on the night of his murder. Photo: Library of Congress.

The only known view of Lincoln in death. Lincoln lies in state in the rotunda of New York City Hall. As 200,000 people lined up to view the President, Booth was relaxing for the first time in ten days at the home of Richard Garrett near Bowling Green, Virginia. Photo: Illinois State Historical Library, Springfield, Illinois.

MEMENTO MORI.

Born, February 12th, 1809.
Assassinated, April 15th, 1865.

"Just of his Word—Observant of his Right."

Memento Mori. A memento of death. This poster was one of many that were displayed throughout the North in memory of Lincoln. Few survive today and are sought after as mementos of the assassination.

SELECTED READING LIST

1. Bryan, George S. *The Great American Myth.* Carrick and Evans, Inc., New York. 1940.

2. Clark, Champ. *The Assassination.* Time-Life Books, Alexandria, Virginia. 1987.

3. Congress. *Impeachment Investigation. Testimony Taken Before the Judiciary Committee of the House of Representatives in the Investigation of the Charges Against Andrew Johnson. Second Session, Thirty-ninth Congress, and First Session, Fortieth Congress. 1867.* Government Printing Office, Washington. 1867.

4. Eisenschiml, Otto. *Why Was Lincoln Murdered?* Halcyon House. New York. 1937.

5. Kunhardt, Dorothy Meserve and Philip B. Kunhardt, Jr. *Twenty Days.* Harper & Row, New York. 1965.

6. Pittman, Ben, editor. *The Assassination of President Lincoln and the Trial of the Conspirators.* Funk and Wagnalls, New York. 1954.

7. Poore, Ben Perley, editor. *The Conspiracy Trial for the Murder of the President and the Attempt to Overthrow the Government by the Assassination of its Principal Officers.* 3 vols. J. E. Tilton Company, Boston. 1865. Reprinted by Arno Press, New York Times Company, New York. 1972.

8. Roscoe, Theodore. *The Web of Conspiracy.* Prentice Hall, Inc. Englewood Cliffs, New Jersey. 1959.

9. _____, *From the War Department Files. Statements Made by the Alleged Lincoln Conspirators Under Examination.* 1865. Published by the Surratt Society, Clinton Maryland. 1980.